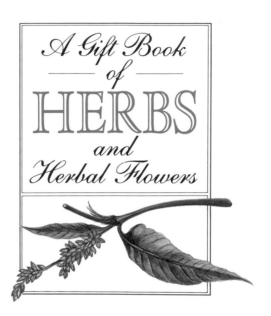

A Gift Book

— of —

HERBS

and

Herbal Flowers

A Gift Book
of
HERBS
and
Herbal Flowers

A collection chosen by
Rosemary Hemphill

WH SMITH
EXCLUSIVE
· BOOKS ·

For my sister-in-law
Sheila Goldie

Contents

*If the day and night are such
that you greet them with joy
and life emits a fragrance
like flowers
and sweet scented herbs—
that is your success.
All nature is your congratulations.*

Henry David Thoreau

INTRODUCTION

The collection of poems, short prose pieces, recipes, craft ideas and folklore in this book is chosen from a wide range of sources where herbs and herbal flowers are the subject. It has been a delightful opportunity to read again the works of inspired men and women, such as the poets of past centuries Andrew Marvell and Longfellow, modern poets like Katharine Tynan and Walter de la Mare, and French writer Colette. Distinguished garden writers with gifts of imagery are Eleanour Sinclair Rohde, Gertrude Jekyll, Frances A. Bardswell and Edna Walling. Practical cooks with creative imaginations are represented by Mrs Beeton, Mrs Leyel, Constance Spry, and today's innovative Elizabeth David. There are therapeutic quotations from antique 'Herballs', old crafts using herbs, and fascinating snippets of herb folklore.

All these writers, and many others, have described in their own particular styles their true appreciation of the simple, yet dynamic, appeal that herbs have — to look at, to smell, taste, and use. Herbs are indeed Earth's gift to all living creatures, and their endurance from time immemorial is expressed in a dictum composed by Andrew Marvell and popular on 17th century sundials:

> *'How could such sweet and wholesome hours*
> *be reckon'd but with herbs and flow'rs.'*

Rosemary Hemphill

Angelica

ngelica is very common in our English gardens; in other places it growes wild without planting, as in Norway, and in an Island of the North called Island, where it groweth very high; it is eaten of the inhabitants, the bark being pilled off, as we understand by some that have travelled into Island, who were sometimes compelled to eat hereof for want of other food; and they report that it hath a good and pleasant taste to them that are hungry. It groweth likewise in divers mountains of Germanie, and especially of Bohemia.

The root of garden Angelica is a singular remedy against poyson, and against the plague, and all infections taken by evill and corrupt aire; if you doe but take a piece of the root and hold it in your mouth, or chew the same between your teeth, it doth most certainely drive away the pestilentiall aire, yea although the corrupt aire have possessed the hart, yet it driveth it out againe, as Rue and Treacle do.

John Gerard, 1597

Borage

Borage for courage! So runs the old proverb. Once sown, you need never sow Borage again; like the Marigolds, it takes care of itself. The starry blue flowers with a cunning dot of black in them are delightful. Blue flowers often have a beauty-patch of black like this. The rough green leaves give an etherealized flavour of cucumber to claret and other cups, and the flowers offer honey to the bees. Our great-great-grandmothers loved to preserve the flowers and candy them for sweetmeats.

Frances A. Bardswell, *The Herb Garden*

15

Excellent herbs had our fathers of old,
Excellent herbs to ease their pain:
Alexanders and marigold,
Eyebright, orris, and elecampane,
Basil, rocket, valerian, rue,
(Almost singing themselves they run),
Vervain, dittany, call-me-to-you,
Cowslip, melilot, rose of the sun,
Anything green that grew out of the mould
Was an excellent herb to our fathers of old.

Mrs C.F. Leyel and Miss Olga Hartley,
The Gentle Art of Cookery, 1930

To make a flower salad, you will need a flat, large, round china or glass platter, or a round tray. On it make a bed of some of the larger herb leaves, for instance angelica, lovage, comfrey, nasturtium, chicory or dandelion. In the centre put a mound of grated carrot, and circle it with small, broken sprigs of washed, raw young cauliflower florets. Next, make a circle of colourful nasturtium flowers interspersed with honeyed bergamot flowers and leaf sprigs, then a surround of alfalfa, or any other favourite sprouts. Around this, make a rainbow circle of sky-blue borage flowers, purple violets, pink or red rose petals, and yellow stars of dill or fennel flowers. Surround the plate with sprays of curly parsley and spearmint tops. If there is still room, add radish 'roses' and crisp curled celery to the flowery platter. Pour a light dressing over all before bearing it to the table. This salad may be made an hour ahead of time and kept fresh in the refrigerator, but do not add the dressing until the very last moment. Not all flowers are edible, so make sure the ones you choose *are*.

Camomile

I love Camomile. The very finely dissected softly green foliage is almost velvety in appearance, and the little daisies are so perky. I most ardently desire a Camomile lawn, and I shall have it one day. Up to the present all that has been achieved outside the vegetable garden is a patch a foot square planted where few grasses will thrive, beneath a Candle bark gum. At least it has proved itself there and made me long all the more to be able to walk across a whole sward of it. It appears that it would take most kindly to the mower and would, I imagine, demand far less mowing than grass (husbands, please note). For the country garden with no water it should prove a boon. It's an *Anthemis*, of course.

Edna Walling, *A Gardener's Log*

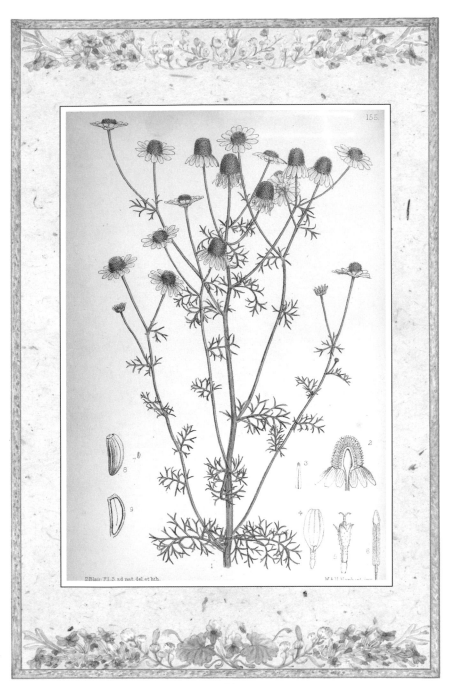

155.

D.Blair F.L.S. ad nat. del. et lith.

M & N Hanhart imp.

21

Chervil

The leaves of sweet Chervill are exceeding good, wholesome and pleasant among other sallad herbs, giving the taste of Anise seed unto the rest.

The seeds eaten as a sallad whiles they are yet green with oile, vineger, and pepper, exceed all other sallads by many degrees, both in pleasantnesse of taste, sweetnesse of smell, and wholsomnesse for the cold and feeble stomacke.

The roots are likewise most excellent in a sallad, if they be boiled and afterwards dressed as the cunning Cooke knoweth better than my selfe: notwithstanding I use to eat them with oile and vineger, being first boiled; which is very good for old people that are dull and without courage: it rejoiceth and comforteth the heart, and increaseth their lust and strength.

John Gerard, 1597

Dandelion

Everybody knows this plant. In May the meadows, filled with the radiant yellow blossoms, can be seen from long distances. The leaves including the roots are eaten as salad. In autumn the roots contain a lot of sugar. Hares, rabbits, birds, and cattle like it very much. The dandelion has existed since the creation of the universe and sows itself.

Father John Künzle,
Herbs and Weeds, 1911

Dill

Few, I imagine, have the least idea what Dill, Coriander, Caraway, or Anise look like when growing. Yet these four aromatic Herbs, although of Eastern origin, do well in English gardens if given a sunny place. They grew quite happily in my breezy garden, where they flowered and went to seed.

Dill, *Anethum graveolens*, turned out to be a lively-looking upright sort of plant, with umbels of pretty yellow flowers. The taste of the seeds is an odd blend of different spices. The name Dill is said to be derived from a Norse word that means to 'dull', or from the Saxon verb *dilla*, to 'lull,' because the seeds are soporific, and used to be given to little babies to make them sleep.

Dill, for infants, is still in fashion. Our village chemist tells us he is always selling it in 'pennorths' for mothers to keep their babies quiet with; but if I set up a still to make Dill-water for them myself, I shall be prosecuted! In cookery, the leaves may be added to fish or mixed with pickled cucumber to 'give the cold fruit a pretty spicie taste.' Of old it was a favourite herb in magic:

> 'Here holy Vervain, and here Dill,
> 'Gainst witchcraft much availing.'

Frances A. Bardswell, *The Herb Garden*

Dill

Elderflower

Elderflower and Gooseberry Syrup

This is a delicious syrup tasting quite definitely of muscatel grapes, and it is described in some books as a muscat syrup. It makes the most delicious water-ice and is useful for flavouring fruit salads and summer drinks. For keeping purposes it must be sterilized after it is bottled. The best bottles to use are those now sold for the purpose with rubber stoppers and clips.

4 lb gooseberries, topped and tailed
3 lb sugar
1 pint water
12 heads of elderflower

Put sugar and water into a pan, when sugar is dissolved add gooseberries, simmer very gently 5–10 minutes. Add washed elderflowers tied in a muslin bag. Allow to infuse until the syrup is well flavoured. Turn into a nylon sieve or muslin bag and allow to drain thoroughly. Strain again through a piece of muslin, pour into bottles and sterilize for 10 minutes. The remaining pulp may be used for gooseberry fool or for a fruit cheese.

Constance Spry and Rosemary Hume, *The Constance Spry Cookery Book*

Fennel

Above the lowly plants it towers,
The fennel, with its yellow flowers,
And in an earlier age than ours
Was gifted with the wondrous powers,
Lost vision to restore.

It gave new strength, and fearless mood;
And gladiators, fierce and rude,
Mingled it in their daily food;
And he who battled and subdued,
A wreath of fennel wore.

Longfellow, 'The Goblet of Life'

He who sees fennel and gathers it not,
is not a man but a devil.

Welsh Mydvai, 13th century

Foxglove

Strange, this objection to plants that readily sow themselves about the garden! One hears so many say, "Foxgloves are such a nuisance; they come up all over the garden," and they do in mine, but never yet have there been too many; never yet enough! And with foxgloves it is such fun: they are sticklers about the "Rotation of Crops!" If you have had a marvellous show in one corner of the garden one year, you need not imagine a similar display there the following year; for they will most probably have marched off to another part, and where you had never thought of planting them they will quietly send up their little spires and say, "Here we are! How do we look in this setting?" Of course, you cannot expect to have all these delightful surprises in a garden that is regularly spaded over the minute some crop is past its best. A garden should, I always feel, be just a little too big to keep the whole cultivated, then it has a chance to go a little wild in spots, and make some pictures for you. Hand weeding is the only safe way to deal with these wild bits, carefully removing weeds only, and allowing the self-sown foxgloves, cyno-glossums, columbines, sweet williams, and forget-me-nots to fight it out among themselves.

Edna Walling, *A Gardener's Log*

It is a commendable and seemely thing to behold out at a window manie acres of ground well tilled and husbanded, whether it be a Medow, a Plot for planting of Willowes, or arable ground . . . but yet it is much more to behold faire and comely Proportions, handsome and pleasant Arbors, and, as it were, Closets, delightfull borders of Lavender, Rosemarie, Boxe and other such like: to heare the ravishing musicke of an infinite number of pretie small Birds, which continually, day and night, doe chatter and chant their proper and naturall branch-songs upon the Hedges and Trees of the Garden; and to smell so sweet a Nose-gay so neare at hand; seeing that this so fragrant a smell cannot but refresh the Lord of the Farme exceedingly, when going out of his bed-chamber in the morning after the Sunne-rise, and whiles as yet the cleare and pearle-like dew doth pearche unto the grasse, he giveth himself to heare the melodious musicke of the Bees; which busying themselves in gathering of the same, doe also fill the ayre with a most acceptable sweet and pleasant harmonie: besides the borders and continued Rowes of soveraigne Thyme, Balme, Rosemarie, Marjerome, Cypers, Soothernwood, and other fragrant hearbes, the sight and view whereof cannot but give great contentment to the beholder.

Richard Surflet, *The Countrey Farme*, 1600

Much of the old lore has been lost, and patent medicines have been allowed to usurp the place of the herbal teas; but at last herbs are coming into their own again, and we are beginning to realise our folly in making so little use of them, and especially of the sun-loving aromatic herbs. The mere scent of them is a tonic, and even in winter their leaves give one a delicious reminder of sunshine and joyous vitality.

Eleanour Sinclair Rohde,
A Garden of Herbs

Garlic

Wel loved he garleek, oynons, and eek lekes,
And for to drynken strong wyn, reed as blood.

Chaucer, *The Canterbury Tales*

Mars owns this herb. This was anciently accounted the poor man's treacle, it being a remedy for all diseases and hurts (except those which itself breeds.) It . . . helps the biting of mad dogs, and other venomous creatures; kills the worms in children, cuts and voids tough phlegm, purges the head, helps the lethargy, is a good preservative against, and a remedy for, any plague, sore, or foul ulcer; takes away spots and blemishes in the skin, eases pains in the ears, ripens and breaks imposthumes, or other swellings; and for all those diseases the onions are as effectual . . . It is also held good in hydropic diseases, the jaundice, falling-sickness, cramps, convulsions, the piles or hemorrhoids, or other cold diseases. Authors quote many other diseases this is good for; but conceal its vices. Its heat is very vehement; and all vehement hot things send up but ill-savoured vapours to the brain. In choleric men it will add fuel to the fire; in men oppressed by melancholy, it will attenuate the humour, and send up strong fancies, and as many strange visions to the head; therefore let it be taken inwardly with great moderation; outwardly you may make more bold with it.

Nicholas Culpepper, 17th century

Alca.

39

Hyssop

Cleane Hysop *is an hearbe to purge and clense*
Raw flegmes, and hurtfull humours from the brest,
The same unto the lungs great comfort lends,
With hony boyl'd: but farre above the rest
It gives good colour, and complexion mends,
And is therefore with women in request.

Sir John Harington, *The Englishmans Doctor*, 1607

Purge me with Hyssop, and I shall be clean;
Wash me, and I shall be whiter than snow.

Psalms 51,7

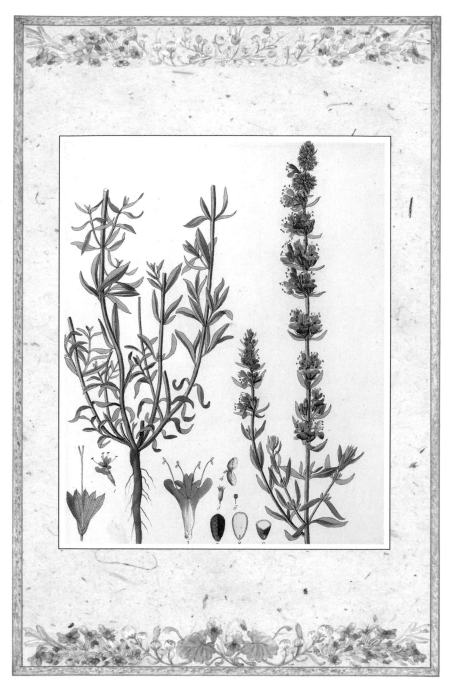

41

When skies are blue and days are bright
A kitchen-garden's my delight,
Set around with rows of decent box
And blowsy girls of hollyhocks.

Lavender, sweet-briar, orris. Here
Shall Beauty make her pomander,
Her sweet-balls for to lay in clothes
That wrap her as the leaves the rose.

Katharine Tynan, 'The Choice'

The garden should be something without and beyond nature, a page from an old romance, a scene in fairyland, a gateway through which imagination, lifted above the sombre realities of life, may pass into a world of dreams. More than any other kind of garden does the Herb-garden lead us into a region of romance, of mystery and sweet remembrance, yet withal there is a common-sense side to it whose usefulness is not to be denied.

Frances A. Bardswell,
The Herb Garden

Iris florentina

Orris powder is the ground up dried root of the
Iris florentina (Flower-de-luce).

Thou art the Iris, fair among the fairest,
Who, armed with golden rod
And winged with the celestial azure, bearest
The message of some God.

Thou art the Muse, who far from crowded cities
Hauntest the sylvan streams,
Playing on pipes of reed the artless ditties
That come to us as dreams.

O Flower-de-luce, bloom on, and let the river
Linger to kiss thy feet!
O flower of song, bloom on, and make for ever
The world more fair and sweet.

Longfellow, 'Flower-de-luce'

Iris florentina

How well the skilful Gardner drew
Of flow'rs and herbes this Dial new;
Where from above the milder Sun
Does through a fragrant Zodiak run;
And, as it works, th'industrious Bee
Computes its time as well as we.
How could such sweet and wholesome Hours
Be reckon'd but with herbs and flow'rs!

Andrew Marvell, 1621–78

An honest ale-house
where we shall find a cleanly room,
lavender in the windows,
and twenty ballads stuck about the wall.

The Compleat Angler

Lavender Potpourri

1 cup English Lavender flowers
½ cup Marjoram leaves
1 tablespoon Thyme leaves
1 tablespoon Mint leaves
1 tablespoon Orris Root powder
2 teaspoons ground Coriander
¼ teaspoon ground Cloves
a few drops Lavender Oil

Mix the flowers and leaves together.
Blend the orris powder, coriander and cloves separately,
then stir in the lavender oil and add to the dried material.
This mixture can go into sachets or into bowls.

NOTE: The quantities given are for dried
flowers and foliage.

Marigold

Marigold Pudding

Take a pretty quantity of marygold flowers very well shred, mingle with a pint of cream on new milk and almost a pound of beef suet chopt very small, the gratings of a twopenny loaf and stirring all together put it into a bag flower'd and tie it fast. It will be boil'd within an hour — or bake in a pan.

John Evelyn, *Acetaria*, 1699

I shall have many other plants too, rose windows of verbena, pipes of birthwort, powder puffs of thrift, crosses of St Helena's cross, spikes of lupin, night-blooming bindweed, and marvel of Peru, nebulae of bent grass, and clouds of feathered pinks. Beggar's staff to aid the last steps of my journey; asters to fill my nights with stars. Harebells, a thousand harebells to ring at dawn just as the cock starts crowing; a dahlia pleated like a Clouet ruff, a foxglove in case a needy fox should visit me, and a rocket. Not, as you might think, a rocket to send into the sky, but a rocket to edge my flower bed with. Yes, to edge my flower bed with! And for that I need lobelias too, for the blue of the lobelia has no rival either in the sky or in the sea. As for honeysuckle, I shall choose the most delicate, the one that is wan with the burden of its own scent. Finally, I must have a magnolia, a good layer, one that will be covered all over with white eggs when Easter comes; and wistaria that will let its long flowers drip off it one by one till it turns the terrace into a lake of mauve. And some lady's slipper, enough to make shoes for everyone in the house. But no oleanders, if you please. They call the oleander the laurel rose, and I want only laurels and roses.

Colette, *Earthly Paradise*

Mistletoe

M istletoe, which, like holly, has been associated from
time immemorial with Christmas festivities, is one of
the most mysterious plants . . .

In olden times mistletoe was highly valued for its medicinal properties. The ancient Druids esteemed it so highly that
they called it 'all-heal.' Even as late as Elizabethan times
the plant was held in such veneration that when cut for
medicinal purposes it was never allowed to fall to the ground.
Both William Langham, the author of *The Garden of Health*,
and Gerard, the author of the famous *Herbal*, give this
information. Both of those writers state also that the berries,
enclosed in a 'silver tablet,' were worn as amulets to shield
the wearer from falling sickness, and that those suffering
from this illness drank the berries with ravens' eggs. Perhaps
the most curious information about mistletoe is that to be
found in Sir Hugh Platt's *Flores Paradise*. He says: 'By
sitting uppon a hill late in an evening neere a wood, in a fewe
nights a fire-drake will appear; marke where it lighteth, and
there you shall finde an Oake with Mistletoe therein, at the
roote whereof there is a missel child, whereof many strange
things are conceived.' Even in the eighteenth century mistletoe figured largely in folk medicine, being highly esteemed
for epilepsy. Sir George Colbatch, a noted physician, published
in 1719 *A Dissertation Concerning Mistletoe*.

Eleanour Sinclair Rohde, *Gardens of Delight*

Mugwort

And if a Footman take *Mugwort* and put it into his Shoes in the Morning, he may goe forty miles before Noon and not be weary.

William Coles, *The Art of Simpling*, 1656

Eldest of worts
Thou hast might for three
And against thirty
For venom availest
For flying vile things,
Mighty against loathed ones
That through the land rove.

Lacnunga (Saxon Herbal), 10th century

Nasturtium

I sowed a seede thei brought me from the Peru, more to see his fairnesse than for any medicinall vertues that it hath . . . It is a flower very beautiful, which doeth adornate the gardens.

Nicholas Monardes, *Joyfull Newes out of the New Founde Worlde* (trans. Frampton), 1577

The flours are dispersed throughout the whole plant, of colour yellow, with a crossed star overthwart the inside, of a deepe Orange colour: unto the backe-part of the same doth hang a taile or spurre, such as hath the Larkes heele, called in Latine *Consolida Regalis*; but greater, and the spur or heele longer; which beeing past there succeed bunched and knobbed coddes or seed vessells, wherein is contained the seed, rough, browne of colour, and like unto the seeds of the beete, but smaller.

John Gerard, *The Herball*, 1597

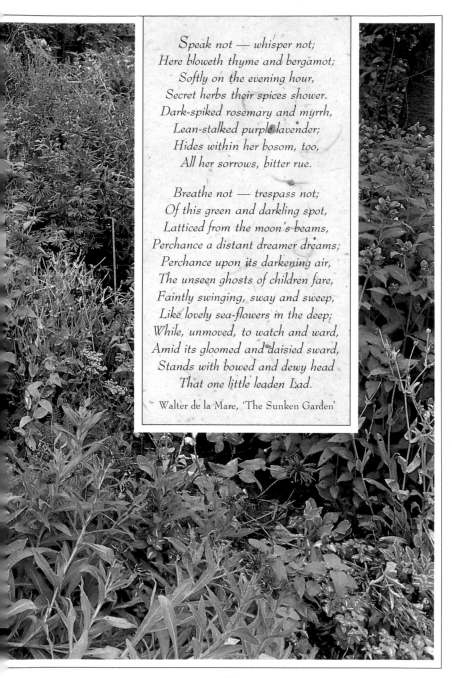

Speak not — whisper not;
Here bloweth thyme and bergamot;
Softly on the evening hour,
Secret herbs their spices shower.
Dark-spiked rosemary and myrrh,
Lean-stalked purple lavender;
Hides within her bosom, too,
All her sorrows, bitter rue.

Breathe not — trespass not;
Of this green and darkling spot,
Latticed from the moon's beams,
Perchance a distant dreamer dreams;
Perchance upon its darkening air,
The unseen ghosts of children fare,
Faintly swinging, sway and sweep,
Like lovely sea-flowers in the deep;
While, unmoved, to watch and ward,
Amid its gloomed and daisied sward,
Stands with bowed and dewy head
That one little leaden Lad.

Walter de la Mare, 'The Sunken Garden'

Parsley

To preserve Parsley through the Winter

Use freshly gathered parsley for keeping, and wash it perfectly free from grit and dirt; put it into boiling water which has been slightly salted and well skimmed, and then let it boil for 2 or 3 minutes; take it out, let it drain, and lay it on a sieve in front of the fire, when it should be dried as expeditiously as possible. Store it away in a very dry place in bottles, and when wanted for use, pour over it a little warm water, and let it stand for about 5 minutes.

Mrs Isabella Beeton, *Household Management*, 1861

Peppermint

Peppermint is one of the most popular Herbs in the garden, for anyone need but pick a leaf and smell it, and at once he knows what it is. If people only knew how good the fresh green leaves are, when bruised and laid upon the aching part to cure nervous headaches, the plant would be liked even better than it is. There is such a curious hot-coldness about Peppermint; it diffuses warmth, yet with it a strange numbness which is soothing. The flowery tops of all Mints contain a certain portion of camphor. Peppermint is reponsible for that modern comfort, menthol—modern to us, that is. The Japanese enjoyed its blessing two hundred years ago, and carried it about in silver boxes hanging from their girdles. Peppermint can easily be distinguished at sight from Spear Mint by its leaves being stalked, also by having a more purplish tinge of colour.

Frances A. Bardswell, *The Herb Garden*

Pink

Here is another plant that has been forsaken by modern medicine on the grounds that it is ineffectual. Yet doctors formerly included it among the cordial plants and employed it with success in the treatment of malignant fevers.

This usage certainly seems to support the story that supposedly led to the introduction of the pink into France: the Saint Louis crusaders, struck down by plague outside Tunis, are said to have drunk a certain aromatic liqueur made with pinks which reputedly alleviated their fever, whereupon they determined to bring back with them some specimens of the plant which had thus relieved their ills — which would explain why the pink was originally called *tunica*, the name also given to the syrup prescribed for persons 'afflicted with very malignant fevers'.

Whatever the advocates of chemically manufactured drugs may say, the pink can still render service for feverish conditions, when it promotes perspiration and quenches the thirst.

The rules laid down by Doctor Chomel still serve as a guide for us to follow: 'Among the great number of species of pink that are grown in gardens, choose those which are simplest in form, and of these the reddest and most fragrant.' The petals are picked and used either fresh to make a syrup or *ratafia*, or dried in the shade to make infusions . . . ; to be taken twice a day).

Jean Palaiseul, *Grandmother's Secrets*

The fairest
flowers
o' the season
are our
carnations, and
streak'd gillyvors
[pinks].

William Shakespeare,
The Winter's Tale

Primrose

As early as January the first primroses shine forth in their ethereal loveliness, but they never attain their full beauty till April sun and showers have developed their soft beautiful leaves. Woodland primroses are such shy flowers that they never look quite at their ease in gardens except in a wild part or on a bank . . . The first ambassadors of spring in the woodlands bring with them a nameless quality from worlds infinitely remote and beyond our ken. Their secret is held in their faint ethereal perfume, so delicate that one never tires of it, so fresh that no other scent can be compared to its unearthly purity. They are redolent of the paths of the angels. Primroses shine with a sudden gladness lacking in flowers far more brilliant in hue. But their light does not seem to be of this earth, and memories of them haunt us even when the merry bluebells carpet the greenwood.

Eleanour Sinclair Rohde, *The Scented Garden*

Herb Vinegars

There are many different uses for the herbs in your garden, so while they are still bountiful, making herb vinegars is a very satisfying and useful task, and they make delightful and unusual gifts. Pick and wash the herbs to be used and dry them on absorbent paper. Pack the leaves into clean bottles or jars with lids, and fill with white wine vinegar, replacing the lids firmly. Stand the infusing vinegars on a sunny windowsill for about two weeks. The warmth from the sun releases the flavour and perfume of the herbs. If there is no sun during this time, let them stand for two more weeks.

Rosemary

Rosemarie, the cheefest beautie of Gardens, and not to be wanted in the Kitchen . . . it is sette by women for their pleasure, to growe in sundry proportions, as in the fashion of a Cart, a Peacock, or such like thing as they fancie.

Barnabe Googe, *Four Books of Husbandry*, 1577

Boyle the leaves in white wine and washe thy face therewith and thy browes and thou shalt have a faire face.

Also put the leaves under the bedde and thou shalt be delivered of all evill dreames.

Smell it oft and it shall keep thee youngly.

Bancke's Herball, 1525

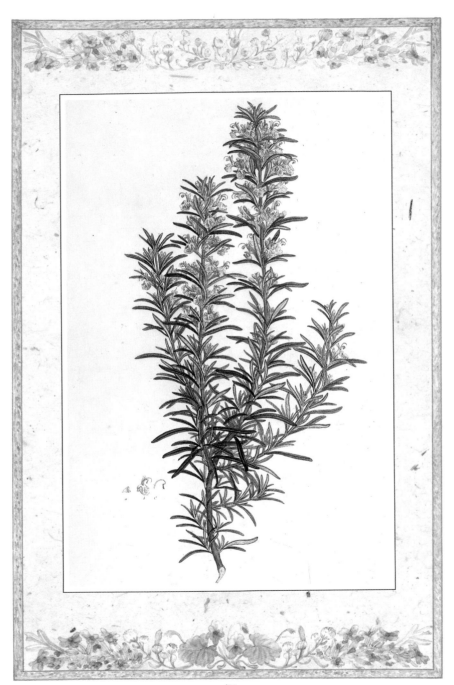

Crystallized herbs and flowers

Whole small blooms, or single petals may be used, the most suitable being violets, borage flowers, rosemary flowers, English primroses, rose petals and small whole rosebuds. (The various scented mint leaves are excellent too.)

Put the white of an egg into a saucer, break it up with a fork, but do not whip. Take a dry flower, or a single petal, and with a small paintbrush dipped into the egg white, cover it completely, then shake caster sugar through a fine sieve over the flower, first on one side, then the other. As they are finished, spread them out on greaseproof paper laid in a small oven dish. Put the flowers in a very slow oven with the door open for approximately 10–15 minutes, gently turning them as the sugar hardens. Do not leave too long or they will go brown. Store the candied flowers between layers of greaseproof paper in an airtight box.

Rue

Herb of Grace

Find some freckled fern seed to sprinkle in your shoes
And you may step invisible down the peopled street,
Or curve about the apple boughs like swallows if you choose,
Lifted by the elfin wings that tingle in your feet.
Oh, you may cull a-many sweet with fern seed in your shoe!
But leave alone the rue,—
Little boy, little girl,
Leave alone the rue!

Keep the downy dittany and storms will bring you calm,
Fill a vervain pillow for a thought-grieved head;
Cherish balm whene'er you can, there's none too much of balm,
And never stop for rosemary, 'twill follow where you tread.
Taste the scarlet love-apple, if youth will drive you to,
But leave alone the rue —
Fair lass, fine lad,
Leave alone the rue!

Mix tansy in your Easter cake and earn a placid year,
For though you cross the Little Folk they cannot then offend;
Give a spray and take a spray of ivy from your dear,
But pay with coin for parsley, or its price will be a friend.
Wear a four-leafed clover and the charm will win you through;
But leave alone the rue —
Grave man, wise woman,
Leave alone the rue!

Lovelier than wealth is laughing potentilla's gold,
Eyebright is beautiful and kind to eyes that weep;
Rich herbs of healing the wild glens hold
With hemlock and foxglove for those sick for sleep.
Surely there are flowers enough and strong leaves too!
Must you gather rue?
Poor things, poor things,
Leave alone the rue!

Anon

Saffron

'I must have Saffron to colour the warden pies,' said the clown to Perdita, who was making pasties for the sheep-shearing, and the same sweet colouring matter enriches the cakes and buns of the present day. We use it, too, in starch for colouring lace and linen; but we do not expect it to cure measles, nor do we stuff pillows and cushions with it with a view to its animating and restorative qualities. Nowadays, if one is in a merry mood, none of his friends would say of him, 'He has slept in a sack of Saffron.'

As children, when it was the fashion to keep canary-birds, how many a pinch of saffron—most fascinating to play with—would be begged for, to put in their drinking-water! We were confident it would not only improve the colour of their feathers, but would also give our dickies vigour and strength while moulting. The dye is such a lovely rich shade, and colours the water at once. It will dye the hair, too, magnificently. King Henry the Eighth forbade its use for this purpose. In Ireland women sometimes wash their sheets in Saffron-water, thinking to strengthen their limbs.

Nobody has ever praised Saffron more warmly than Sir Francis Bacon. 'Saffron conveys medicine to the heart,' he said, 'cures its palpitation, removes melancholy and uneasiness, revives the brain, renders the mind cheerful, and generates boldness.' Another remark of his was that 'What made the English people sprightly was the liberal use of Saffron in their broths and sweetmeats.'

Frances A. Bardswell, *The Herb Garden*

LE SAFRAN

Sage

'Sir' John Hill, who had a famous garden in Bayswater during the latter half of the eighteenth century, tells us in his *Vertues of British Herbs*, that the chief goodness of sage was to be found in the sage flowers when they begin to open. 'Just when the flowers of sage begin to open there is in their cups a fragrant resin, highly flavoured, balmy, delicate, and to the taste one of the most delicious cardials that can be thought, warm and aromatic . . . Sage properly prepared will retard that rapid progress of decay that treads upon our heels so fast in the latter years of life, will preserve the faculties and memory, more valuable to the rational mind than life itself without them; and will relieve that faintness, strengthen that weakness, and prevent absolutely that sad depression of spirits, which age often feels and always fears, which will long prevent the hands from trembling, and the eyes from dimness and make the lamp of life, so long as nature lets it burn, burn brightly.'

Eleanour Sinclair Rohde, *The Scented Garden*

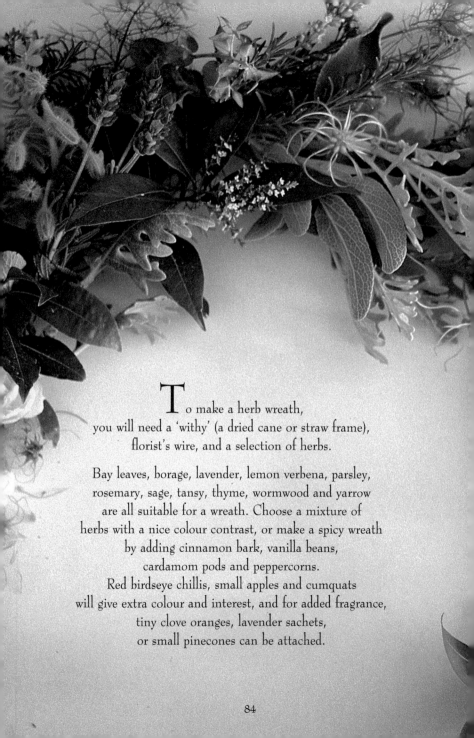

To make a herb wreath,
you will need a 'withy' (a dried cane or straw frame),
florist's wire, and a selection of herbs.

Bay leaves, borage, lavender, lemon verbena, parsley,
rosemary, sage, tansy, thyme, wormwood and yarrow
are all suitable for a wreath. Choose a mixture of
herbs with a nice colour contrast, or make a spicy wreath
by adding cinnamon bark, vanilla beans,
cardamom pods and peppercorns.
Red birdseye chillis, small apples and cumquats
will give extra colour and interest, and for added fragrance,
tiny clove oranges, lavender sachets,
or small pinecones can be attached.

Wire together several sprigs of herbs and form
into bunches. Attach the first bunch to
the frame with florist's wire by twisting
the wire around the frame. Add the
next bunch in the same way so
that it overlaps the first bunch.

Continue until the frame
is covered, making sure
that all the bunches curve
in the same direction.
Attach a loop of florist's
wire to the back of
the wreath for hanging.

Southernwood

I'll give to him,
Who gathers me, more sweetness than he'd dream
Without me — more than any lily could.
I that am flowerless, being Southernwood.
Shall I give you honesty,
Or lad's love to wear?
Or a wreath less fair to see,
Juniper or Rosemary?
Flaxenhair.

Rosemary, lest you forget,
What was lief and fair,
Lad's love, sweet thro' fear and fret,
lad's love, green and living yet,
Flaxenhair

Finnish Bride Song

Tansy

In busy kitchens, in olden days,
Tansy was used in a score of ways;
Chopped and pounded, when cooks would make
Tansy puddings, and tansy cake,
Tansy posset, or tansy tea;
Physic or flavouring tansy'd be.
People who know
Have told me so!

That is my tale of the past; today,
Still I'm here by the King's Highway,
Where the air from the fields is fresh and sweet,
With my fine-cut leaves and my flowers neat.
Were ever such button-like flowers seen—
Yellow, for elfin coats of green?
Three in a row—
I stitch them so!

Cicely M. Barker

Tarragon

Poulet à l'estragon

A simple version of chicken cooked with tarragon, one of the nicest of chicken dishes, and essentially a summer one, as it can be successfully made only with fresh tarragon.

Work a tablespoon of chopped tarragon leaves with 2 oz. of butter, season with salt and pepper, and stuff a 3-lb. roasting chicken with this mixture. Cook the chicken in butter in a thick, covered casserole. The bird should be laid on its side, not breast upwards, and should be turned over half-way through the cooking, and basted now and again with the tarragon-flavoured butter which comes out of it.

When it is tender remove to a serving dish and stir into the juices in the pan a walnut of butter worked with a teaspoon of flour. When this has amalgamated, add ¼ pint of cream and 2 tablespoons of chopped tarragon. Bring to the boil and when it has thickened pour it over the chicken.

Elizabeth David, *Summer Cooking*

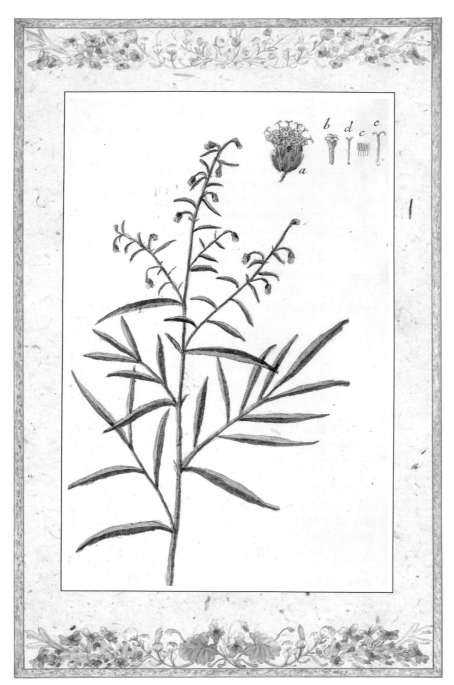

91

It is much better for the cook to go out and compose the little *bouquet* for the special flavouring of some delicate soup or sauce, picking the right quantity and proportion straight from the fragrant growing things. Moreover, having them all before her, she has a better chance of getting a knowledge of their natures and separate identities, and the little plants and their ways and uses must necessarily acquire in her eyes a more distinctly living interest.

Gertrude Jekyll, *Home and Garden*

Thyme

To enable one to see the Fairies

A pint of sallet oyle and put it into a vial glasse; and first wash it with rose-water and marygolde water; the flowers to be gathered towards the east. Wash it till the oyle becomes white, then put into the glasse, and then put thereto the budds of hollyhocke, the flowers of marygolde, the flowers or toppes of wild thyme, the budds of young hazle, and the thyme must be gathered neare the side of a hill where fairies use to be; and take the grasse of a fairy throne; then all these put into the oyle in the glasse and sette it to dissolve three dayes in the sunne and then keep it for thy use.—Receipt dated 1600.

Eleanour Sinclaire Rohde, *A Garden of Herbs*

A fit playground for fairies which are said to love thyme-decked banks for their revels, although we confess we have never been so fortunate as to see even one.

from Edna Walling, *A Gardener's Log*

Thymus Serpyllum.

The wholesome sage, and lavender still gray
Ranke smelling rue, and cummin good for eyes
The roses, reigning in the pride of May
Sharp hishop, good for greens woundes remedies.
Fair marigolds, and bees alluring thyme,
Sweet marjoram, and daysies in their prime,
Cool violets, and Alpine growing still,
Embalmed balm, and cheerful galingale,
Dull popie, and drink quickning setual,
Veyne-healing verven, and head purging dill
Sound savorie, and basil harti-hale,
Fat coleworts, and comforting parsline,
Colde lettuce, and refreshing rosemarie,
And whatso else of vertue, good or ill,
Grew in this garden, fetched from far away
Of everyone, he takes and tastes at will.

Edmund Spenser, 'The Fate of the Butterfly'

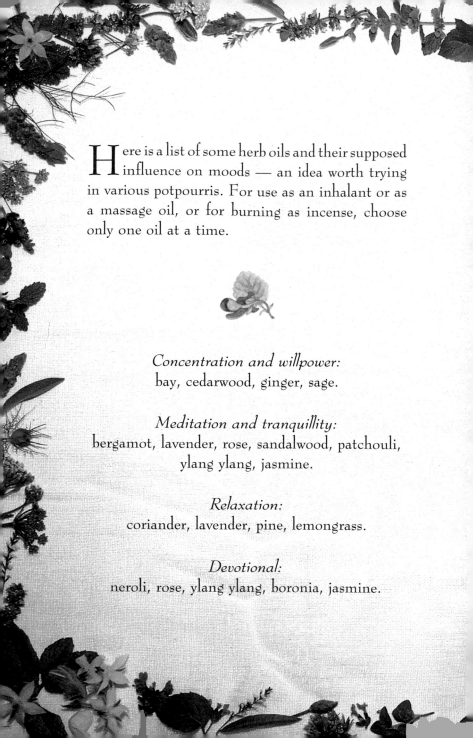

Here is a list of some herb oils and their supposed influence on moods — an idea worth trying in various potpourris. For use as an inhalant or as a massage oil, or for burning as incense, choose only one oil at a time.

Concentration and willpower:
bay, cedarwood, ginger, sage.

Meditation and tranquillity:
bergamot, lavender, rose, sandalwood, patchouli, ylang ylang, jasmine.

Relaxation:
coriander, lavender, pine, lemongrass.

Devotional:
neroli, rose, ylang ylang, boronia, jasmine.

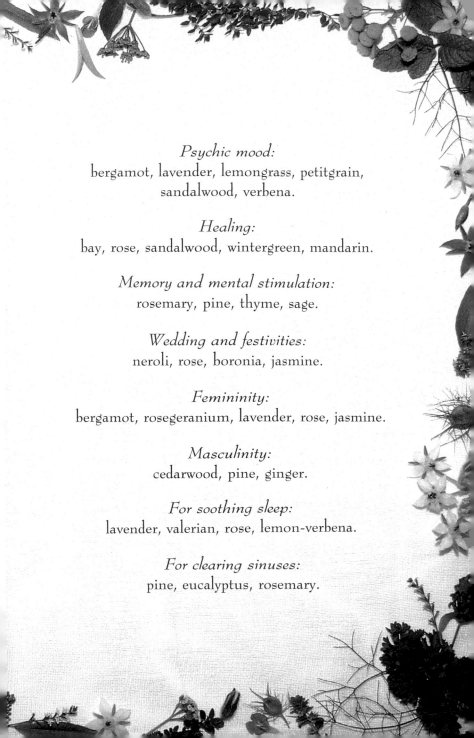

Psychic mood:
bergamot, lavender, lemongrass, petitgrain,
sandalwood, verbena.

Healing:
bay, rose, sandalwood, wintergreen, mandarin.

Memory and mental stimulation:
rosemary, pine, thyme, sage.

Wedding and festivities:
neroli, rose, boronia, jasmine.

Femininity:
bergamot, rosegeranium, lavender, rose, jasmine.

Masculinity:
cedarwood, pine, ginger.

For soothing sleep:
lavender, valerian, rose, lemon-verbena.

For clearing sinuses:
pine, eucalyptus, rosemary.

There are several ways of drying your own herbs. If you are drying them for their aromatic foliage, a general rule is to gather them on a dry day, before noon, when they are at their peak. After that, the sun will have drawn up most of the aromatic essences. Early autumn, just before flowering, is the usual time for harvesting.

The simplest way to dry herbs is to bundle them together neatly in bunches, tie with string or raffia, and hang them in an airy, shady, dust-free place until brittle. Then, strip off the leaves and put them into clean, airtight containers; do not use plastic, it causes 'sweating'.

For really efficient, natural drying, branchlets of herbs can be laid on airy, mesh trays in a warm, dry atmosphere where the air can circulate around them. Spreading the herbs on sheets of clean newspaper and leaving them in a shady area is also an excellent method. If the leaves are the type that retain moisture, to prevent mould or mildew from forming, place them so that they do not have any contact with each other. Never dry foliage in the sun, it will draw out all the flavour; neither should they be dried in a *hot* oven. A warm oven is satisfactory provided the leafy stalks are constantly turned and carefully watched.

Violet

A violet breath,
that opes with magic key
The inmost chambers
of my heart,
And sets its sweetest
mem'ries free.

19th century valentine poem

103

Wormwood

While Wormwood hath seed, get a handful of
twaine,
To save against March, to make flea to refrain:
When chamber is sweep'd, and Wormwood is
strown,
No flea, for his life, dare abide to be known.
What savour is better, if Physic be true,
For places infected than Wormwood or Rue?
It is a comfort for heart and the brain,
And therefore to have it, it is not in vain.

Thomas Tusser, *Five hundred points*, 1573

For the lips of a loose woman drip honey,
and her speech is smoother than oil;
but in the end she is bitter as wormwood,
sharp as a two-edged sword.

Proverbs, 5.3–4

Yarrow

Achilles Yarrow or noble Milfoile, hath a thicke rough roote, with strings fastened thereto; from which immediately rise up divers stalkes, very greene and crested, whereupon do growe long leaves composed of many small jagges, cut even to the middle rib: the flowers stand at the top of the stalkes in spokie umbles or tufts, of a yellowish colour, and pleasant smell.

It is a principall herbe for all kinde of bleedings, and to heale up new and old ulcers and greene wounds.

The plant *Achilles* is thought to be the very same, wherewith *Achilles* cured the wounds of his soldiers.

John Gerard, *The Herball*, 1597

Yarroway, yarroway, bear a white blow
If my love loves me, my nose will bleed now.
If my love don't love me, it won't bleed a drop,
If my love do love me, 'twill bleed every drop.

East Anglian saying

A poor old Widow in her weeds
Sowed her garden with wild-flower seeds;
Not too shallow, and not too deep,
And down came April — drip — drip — drip.
Up shone May, like gold, and soon
Green as an arbour grew leafy June.
And now all summer she sits and sews
Where willow-herb, comfrey, bugloss blows,
Teasel and tansy, meadowsweet,
Campion, toadflax, and rough hawksbit;
Brown bee orchis, and Peals of Bells;
Clover, burnet, and thyme she smells;
Like Oberon's meadows her garden is
Drowsy from dawn till dusk with bees.
Weeps she never, but sometimes sighs,
And peeps at her garden with bright brown eyes;
And all she has is all she needs —
A poor old Widow in her weeds.

Walter de la Mare, 'A Widow's Weeds'

ACKNOWLEDGMENTS

The Publisher would like to thank copyright holders for permission
to reproduce the extracts in this book.

p 12   from *Leaves from Gerard's Herball*,
arr. Marcus Woodward, Thorsons Publishing Group,
HarperCollins Publishers Ltd

p 14   A. & C. Black (Publishers) Limited

p 16   Chatto & Windus, Random Century Group

p 20   Barbara Barnes

p 22   from *Leaves from Gerard's Herball*,
arr. Marcus Woodward, Thorsons Publishing Group,
HarperCollins Publishers Ltd

p 26   A. & C. Black (Publishers) Limited

p 28   J.M. Dent & Sons Ltd Publishers

p 32   Barbara Barnes

p 37   Longman Group UK Limited

p 42   Collins/Angus & Robertson

p 45   A. & C. Black (Publishers) Limited

p 54   Martin Secker & Warburg Ltd, Octopus Publishing Group
(Reed International Books)

p 56   Longman Group UK Limited

p 63   The Literary Trustees of Walter de la Mare and The Society of Authors

p 66   A. & C. Black (Publishers) Limited

p 68   Editions Robert Laffont

p 70   Longman Group UK Limited

p 80   A. & C. Black (Publishers) Limited

p 82   Longman Group UK Limited

p 88   'The Song of the Tansy Fairy' by Cicely Mary Barker;
Frederick Warne & Co., Penguin Books Ltd

p 90   David Higham Associates

p 93   Antique Collectors' Club, Woodbridge, Suffolk, England

p 94   Longman Group UK Limited *(top)*, Barbara Barnes *(bottom)*

p111   The Literary Trustees of Walter de la Mare and The Society of Authors

Pictures

Thanks are due to Trisha Dixon for taking the photographs
on pages *36–7, 84–5, 92–3, 98–9, 100–1*

The Bridgeman Art Library
pp 24–25, 33, 53, 71

E.T. Archive
pp 15, 21, 29, 31, 39, 41, 65, 75, 83, 87, 91, 95, 105

Elizabeth Whiting & Associates, London
p 55

Fine Art Photographic Library Ltd
pp 4–5, 6, 10, 57, 61, 102–3, 108–9

Jerry Harpur
pp 35, 43

Insight Picture Library
pp 8–9 (Linda Burgess), *16–17* (Linda Burgess),
44–5 (Linda Burgess), *49* (Linda Burgess),
72–3 (Michelle Garrett), *112*

Mary Evans Picture Library
pp 13, 23, 27, 79

S. & O. Matthews
pp 2–3

National Trust Photographic Library
pp 62–3 (Neil Campbell-Sharp),
96–7 (Stephen Robson)

Retrograph Archive
p 81

Angelo Hornak
pp 47, 59 , 67, 107

Amoret Tanner Collection
p 69

Tessa Traeger, Rosetti Studios
pp 19, 77

This edition produced exclusively in the UK for WH Smith Ltd
Greenbridge Road, Swindon SN3 3LD.

A Kevin Weldon Production

Published by Weldon Publishing
a division of Kevin Weldon & Associates Pty Limited
372 Eastern Valley Way, Willoughby, NSW 2068, Australia

First Published 1991

Design: Michele Withers
Picture research: Jane Lewis
Illustrations: Barbara Rodanska
Typeset in Bernhard Modern by Savage Type, Brisbane, Australia
Printed in Hong Kong by South China Printing Company (1988) Limited

National Library of Australia Cataloguing-in-Publication data
A gift book of herbs and herbal flowers.
ISBN 1 86302 132 9.
1. Herbs — Gift books. I. Hemphill, Rosemary.
641.357